Measuring Time

Days of the Week

Tracey Steffora

Heinemann Library
Chicago, Illinois

www.heinemannraintree.com
Visit our website to find out more information about Heinemann-Raintree books.

To order:
☎ Phone 888-454-2279
▣ Visit www.heinemannraintree.com to browse our catalog and order online.

Edited by Tracey Steffora and Dan Nunn
Designed by Richard Parker
Picture research by Hannah Taylor
Originated by Capstone Global Library Ltd
Printed and bound in the United States of America,
North Mankato, MN

14 13 12
10 9 8 7 6 5 4 3

Library of Congress Cataloging-in-Publication Data
Steffora, Tracey.
  Days of the week / Tracey Steffora.
    p. cm.—(Measuring time)
  Includes bibliographical references and index.
  ISBN 978-1-4329-4901-3 (hc)—ISBN 978-1-4329-4908-2 (pb) 1.
Time—Juvenile literature. 2. Days—
Juvenile literature. 3. Week—Juvenile literature. 4. Time
measurement—Juvenile literature. I. Title.
  QB209.5.S745 2011
  529'.1—dc22

                    2010028870

062012
006758RP

Acknowledgments
We would like to thank the following for permission to reproduce photographs: Alamy Images pp. **4** (©Glowimages RM), **8** (©DCPhoto), **14** (©Radius Images), **15** (©Golden Pixels LLC), **18** (©Image Source), **19** (©Blue Jean Images), **20** (©Ana Maria Marques), **23 top** (©DCPhoto); Getty Images p. **13** (Bounce); istockphoto pp. **5** (©Winston Davidian), **9** (©stockcom), **12** (©Rudyanto Wijaya), **23 bot** (©stockcom); Photolibrary pp. **6** (Monkey Business Images Ltd), **7** (Monkey Business Images Ltd), **16** (Banana Stock), **17** (Tom Salyer).

Front cover photograph of calendar days reproduced with permission of Getty Images (Steve McAlister). Back cover photograph of a woman and her daughter shopping for apples reproduced with permission of Photolibrary (Monkey Business Images Ltd).

Every effort has been made to contact copyright holders of any material reproduced in this book. Any omissions will be rectified in subsequent printings if notice is given to the publisher.

Contents

What Is Time?

Time is how long something takes.

Time is when things happen.

We measure time in many ways.

Measuring Time

hour

We measure time in hours.

A long walk can take an hour.

A trip to the store can take an hour.

We measure time in days.

There are 24 hours in a day.

Each day has a morning.

Each day has an evening.

March						
Sunday	Monday	Tuesday	Wednesday	Thursday	Friday	Saturday
		1	2	3	4	5
6	7	8	9	10	11	12
13	14	15	16	17	18	19
20	21	22	23	24	25	26
27	28	29	30	31		

week

We measure time in weeks.

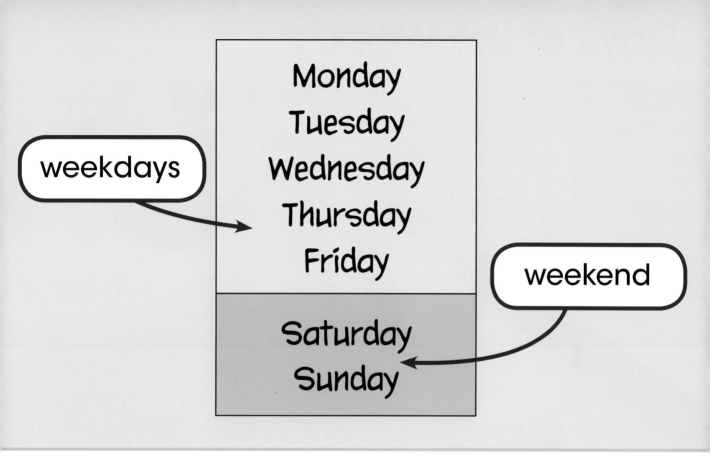

There are 7 days in a week.

Days of the Week

The days of the week help us plan.

Monday   Tuesday   Wednesday   Thursday   Friday

Monday is the first weekday.

This girl visits a library on Monday.

Monday **Tuesday** Wednesday Thursday Friday

This woman goes to the market on Tuesday.

Monday Tuesday **Wednesday** Thursday Friday

These children have dance class on Wednesday.

Monday   Tuesday   Wednesday   **Thursday**   Friday

These children play ball on Thursday.

Monday   Tuesday   Wednesday   Thursday   **Friday**

Friday is the last day of the week.

It is time for the weekend.

This family visits a farm on Saturday.

This family shares a meal on Sunday.
Soon it will be time for a new week!

17 Wed

18 Thu

19 Fri

20 Sat

21 Sun

22 Mon

23 Tue

A calendar shows us the days of the week.

Sunday	Monday	Tuesday	Wednesday	Thursday	Friday	Saturday
?	?	?	?	?	?	?

What do you do each day of the week?

Talking About Time

yesterday today tomorrow

Today is the day it is right now.

Yesterday was the day before today.

22 Tomorrow is the day after today.

Picture Glossary

morning the first part of the day

evening the end of the day

Index

Note to Parents and Teachers

Before reading

With children, identify the current day of the week. Discuss the day that came before today, and the day that comes after today. It is important for children to continue to develop a sense of sequencing as well as build time-order vocabulary (e.g., today, tomorrow, yesterday, before, after, first, next, last).

After reading

Have children discuss what they do on different days of the week. Chart their responses on a timeline or encourage them to make their own books about the days of the week.